WasiWorks Publishing
201(

D1028466

THE EBULLIENCE DISQUISITION:
A Primer On Energy Recognition and Self-Realization

Written by: Odalo M. Wasikhongo

THE EBULLIENCE DISQUISITION:
A Primer On Energy Recognition and Self-Realization
By: Odalo M. Wasikhongo

Table Of Contents:

Introduction

1. Formless-to-Form, Unseen-to-Seen, and Unknown-to-Known

2. Mind Into Matter: All Is Mental

3. Energy Into Mass

4. Ennead: The Ra Creation Story

5. The Human Being As A Light Body

6. Human Response To Vibration

7. How Imprinting Crystals Occurs

8. Keeping Crystals

   How To Clear Crystals

9. How To Program A Crystal

10. Astrologics: Cosmology and Humanity

11. Brainwave Activity & Breath Control: Keys to Your Inner Portals

12. Reiki

13. Cultivating and Nurturing Your Chi Energy

14. Digest: Self-Actualize Now

INTRODUCTION

First and foremost I give Thanks to Great Spirit, the Divine Creative Force, for my life experience, which has brought me into the Light of all the information presented here within these pages. I give thanks for ALL my teachers who have shared their Light and wisdom and teachings with me over the years throughout my growth and development in this lifetime, and all my teachers throughout all lifetimes whose wisdom has contributed to this book. This book, 'The Ebullience Disquisition: A Primer on Energy Recognition and Self-Realization' is exactly what the title describes; it is an introductory work to the recognizing of energy patterns, rhythms, cycles, and synchronicities so that one may recognize the energy of oneself, as well as the energy outside the self (i.e. nature, other people, atmospheres, etc.) to utilize and/or manipulate the recognized patterns to use the energy (pattern, cycle, etc.) to benefit the individual as well the greater good of all concerned. This book hints to a beginning point of energy awareness, how one can become aware of subtle energy, how to use subtle energy to benefit ones health and environment, as well how to recognize patterns formulating when things begin to go out of sync and you want to correct the current. Within these paper walls lies keys to doors opening to many dimensions with you... teachings of the ancient sciences of how to align with Universal Energy to create a harmonious lifestyle, open deeper to awareness, stimulate healing on all levels, as well gain an introductory working knowledge base provided with keys and leads for further studies. You couldn't have come across this book at a better time! A tool you will come back to time and time again. Enjoy!

Odalo M. Wasikhongo

Lesson 1

FORMLESS TO FORM...
UNSEEN TO SEEN...
UNKNOWN TO KNOWN...

"So we fix our eyes not on what is seen, but on what is unseen, since what is seen is temporary, but what is unseen is eternal." ~ 2 Corinthians 4:18

All things in the physical dimension go from formless to form, unseen to seen, unknown to known, and boundless to bound. We see this cyclical pattern play out in nature in every facet of this physical dimension; As a baby goes from an unformed state as an embryo, to a fully formed baby in the mothers womb, we see this pattern. As a baby goes from the darkness in the mother's womb, to the light of the world, we see this cycle. As a baby goes from not knowing how to communicate and integrate into this world, to knowing how to navigate, elevate and manipulate this world and everything in it, we see this pattern play out. As ones eyes constantly open and close, going from darkness to light, we see the pattern of darkness to light consistently play out as a constant reminder...taking notice to how essential it is for our eyes to "rest in peace" regularly every so many hours...serving as a constant reminder of our Source and solace and origin in blackness. In creation, we see ideas go from the mind of individuals and groups to eventually being manifested in the tangible world, showing and proving how all things go from unseen to seen, formless to form, as well as unknown to ones self, and the world, to being known and recognized by all who perceive it. As objects and organisms come into physical manifestation, all things go from infinite to finite, unlimited to limited, timeless to temporary...here one day, and gone the next. So appreciation is vitally important, and key, to enjoying, prospering and entering atmospheres of love and truth, internally and externally, along this divine beautiful journey we call Life. The way in which the mind controls the brain and body shows how the formless expresses itself in, and through, the form. In agriculture, and in nature, we observe how seeds are planted and germinated within the darkness of soil, below the surface and out of sight of the light. As the seeds take root and gain sustenance from the darkness of its surroundings it begins to grow above ground, reaching towards the light, manifesting into a full grown tree, exposing how all seeds planted (be they mental, physical, spiritual, and/or emotional) go from unseen to seen, darkness to light. And just as we see things go from formless to form, we see those same forms return back to formlessness; as kingdoms rise and fall, people are born and pass on, current activities and events become past memories...and ultimately our entire life experience is experienced through a reflection...a memory... it may happen rather quickly, and/or in some cases seemingly continuously...however, it is all experienced as a reflection of what we are currently perceiving mixed in combination with our emotions and experiences, along with the possibilities of the usefulness of that which we are perceiving, which contributes to what we address as the "current moment". Therefore the "current moment" is actually a combination of the so-called past, present, and the potential future observed and reflected upon within the mind. The "current moment" is ultimately an energy current, a current thought-memory, or a current idea being reflected upon within the mind. Life in this physical dimension of duality is essentially a continuous cycle of the same pattern over and over, expressed through a variety and varying degrees of experiences! The universal pattern which is continuously recognized throughout is the cycle of darkness to light, unseen to seen, unknown to known, formless to form, unlimited to limited, etc. Therefore, You, as a being of spirit having a human experience, - as evidenced above with the reference to the necessity of sleep - have the ability to manifest whatever it is, that which is within you, which you have the will power, desire, and ability to create...you can create it!

Lesson 2

MIND INTO MATTER: ALL IS MENTAL

"High energy flowing with the wisdom/ Sense of a rich man, knowledge and the rhythm..." ~ The D.O.C. 'The Formula'

All is Mind, and All is Mental. The Mind of the Infinite is All that is, and It (The Mind of the Infinite) concentrates "Itself" into Magnetism resulting in attractive and repulsive forces which marks the beginning introduction of duality (i.e. contrast opposites; protons and electrons, quarks and leptons, etc.). From Magnetism the Mind further concentrates into Electricity and electric forces (electromagnetic energy), such as Light, Radiation and Ether (Space), which according to Newton's Law of Motion can act upon objects. Electricity is therefore 'charged Energy particles'. Light is a visibly illuminated form of Electricity. The Ether of space and the cosmos is a rarified (meaning, containing less oxygen than usual) and highly elastic substance permeating space, created by the condensation of Light. This Light and Ether further concentrate into Gases and mists in the Ether, in forms such as oxygen, nitrogen, fire, stars, clouds, krypton, nebulas, carbon dioxide etc. Gas is an air-like fluid substance which expands freely to fill any available space regardless of its quantity. The Gases, which then are liquefied by the cold and/or pressure, then flows freely at a constant volume to concentrate and precipitate and congregate into Liquids such as water, acetone, blood, dark matter etc. From Liquid, the Mind further concentrates into a firm and stable shape which is not liquid nor fluid known as a solid...The Mind is concentrated into solid materials such as minerals, earths, amoebas, animals, insects, humanity, planets, etc. The Mind therefore created space to exist, and at the same time It occupies that same space. Of the 7 substances of the Universe, all of which came from out of No apparent Thing (Nothing), but rather originated and manifested itself out of the Mind of God (Universal Conscious Mind). Thus All is Mind, and Consciousness is Vibration. Therefore, from Radiation and vibration of Light and Mind we arrive at particles (i.e. protons, electrons, neutrons, quarks, leptons, etc.) and states of matter (i.e. solids, liquids, gases, electricity, ether/space, etc.). From these various states of matter we derive organisms such as minerals, plants, insects, animals, and humans, whom birth more organisms, continuing life continuously... All of which stem, and are fueled continuously, from Mind. All is Mind. All is mental.

Closely analyzing the above breakdown of Energy-To-Matter, one can begin to recognize a common theme in motion. Spirit is Energy and Energy is Atoms/Cells Vibrating at a specific frequency...That Vibrational Frequency gives birth to Information in Vibration/Motion, also known as Energy-in-Motion or Emotion/Emotional Resonance. Therefore, Matter and the Material World, is quite simply a manifestation of Energy, slowed down extremely (in other words, a dense and slowly vibrating form of information)... All of which is malleable and can be shaped, and re-shaped, by the Mind through Intention...for "Energy follows Intent." And so, mass can change to energy, and energy can change to mass...all of which happens via the interaction of the Four Fundamental Forces of the Universe. The Four Fundamental Forces of the Universe are the *Strong Nuclear Force* which holds quarks and leptons together at the sub-atomic level creating protons and neutrons; the *Electro-Magnetic Force* which acts upon electrically charged particles via photons; then there's the *Weak Nuclear*

Force which is responsible for the radioactivity throughout the universe, which acts upon the electrons, neutrinos, and quarks; then lastly there is the *Gravitational Force* which acts upon all particles with mass, pulling, forming, shifting, shaping and binding matter.

Understanding the fundamental scientific principles of *All is Mind*; *Energy Follows Intent*; *Energy can change to Mass* and *Mass can change to Energy*; *Consciousness is Vibration*; *All the Senses are Vibrations* (vibrational receptors), THEN we can begin to put together the picture of our understanding...that Everything we experience via our physical senses (sight, sound, smell, taste, feel, intuition, etc.) is only but the synchronization of our own internal vibration and awareness with that which is currently being experienced, sensed and/or perceived. All is Vibration. Perception is only a matter of alignment. Experience is always unique to each individual observer/experiencer (the one experiencing) because each observer/experiencer has their own unique vibrational frequency through which they observe/experience. Everything is everything. It is what it is. All experiences are unique to the one experiencing...no experiences are exactly the same, just as no fingerprints are identical to one another.

Lesson 3

ENERGY INTO MASS

"...Created from the Classics/ phenomenal blackbody/ sun radiating oscillating my skin/ enters the One..."
~ Ozon 'Hannibal' on Space Suits EP

Now here, in this portion of the book, the words "Spirit" and "Energy" can be used interchangeably. The human being is a Light Being, also known as a BioPhoton Organism (an organism made of light). This photon (light) energy is the basis of the human body's electromagnetic genetic composition, which vibrates into physical form via the First Law of Energy "Energy can neither be created nor destroyed, only transformed or transferred. The total amount of energy in the universe is constant." The process of energy transforming into matter is explained in the equation:

$E = MC^2$ (or squared)

Meaning...

Energy = Matter x (Speed of Light x Speed of Light)

(OR)

Energy = Matter x (186,000 miles/sec x 186,000 miles/sec)

The key principle that facilitates how energy turns into mass, is by the way energy gains mass when it accelerates. The higher the acceleration the more heavier and dense the mass becomes. So ultimately when we're looking at an object, we are observing the lines of force of an object's energy resistance to acceleration (resistance to motion)...this is known as "Frozen Energy" also called Rest Energy. Matter equals Energy (Spirit) slowed down to dense form. Energy (Spirit) in physical form (Matter) is ultimately atoms (Atum in Kemetic science) vibrating; which in turn means that all things are essentially Energy (Spirit) information (as atoms have intelligence, etc.) coming together in vibrational motion (harmony/alignment), on multiple levels. When Spirit (Energy) accelerates and begins to hit the speed of light, due to the Gamma Factor, the Spirit (Energy) appears to freeze at a point known as the Light Barrier. In this apparent "frozen state" energy begins to pile on and the energy gains mass (photons, light) and begins to take form and shape, based on the molecular structure coding, along the lines of force; in living organisms it's structure and function can be found in the organisms DNA (Deoxyribonucleic Acid). Human beings, living organisms, and all things for that matter, are fundamentally frozen light! The DNA of an organism is the storehouse of information and instructions the organism will need to grow and advance, mature and evolve, and propagate and procreate in this physical dimension. The DNA is therefore pre-coded with a determined idea and/or ultimate program in which it is to manifest and carryout! Thus, an organism does what it does by nature (Natural Law) according to programming, yet all programs are subject to manipulation and/or reprogramming which in turn alters the course and expression of that which is being manipulated. Therefore one thing can be created for the purpose of something specific, but however along the way, can get manipulated and utilized or exercised in a different manner and capacity than initially intended. This happens all the time within society, as we see beautiful people misusing their talents and abilities in a negative way.

The beautiful and magical thing about the DNA is that it is contained within EVERY CELL of the organism! The DNA is a depository of BioPhoton discharge, meaning the DNA is a source of constant light-energy emission. The human organism, as with all living Earthly organisms, emanate a bio-photonic electro-magnetic energy field around them, and the radius of the energy field can expand or contract based on the frequency of the organism. Too high or too low a frequency, or exposure to such frequencies, can give way to imbalance and/or dis-ease in the organism.

This would be a perfect time to present an insightful brief detailed understanding on the Ancient Kemetic (Egyptian) Legend of Ra. Ancient Kemet held a divine culture and community which is far too often misrepresented as a polytheistic culture, or a culture with the belief of many Gods. However in contrast, Ancient Kemet was a culture which embodied divinity and Godhood as a way of life, and should be sought for and found within the individual in search for Truth; using various signs and symbols to bring light and hold reverence and remembrance of our divine nature as spiritual beings living a human experience, and to honor our very existence as a reflection and extension of our divine Creator. The Ancient cultures of Kemet saw God's hand in all of creation, and highlighted and personified the many lessons of nature in the forms of Divine Principles (or so-called "Gods"). The Creation Story of Ra (also known as the Ennead) is a prime example of how high-science of a culture our ancestors, the Kemites, maintained and were so essential to their spiritual systems that their very stories explained clearly how 'things' come into being...so simple it could be made into a story a child could comprehend.

Lesson 4

THE ENNEAD:
RA CREATION STORY

"...Dissect the minds of the nation/ resurrected sages/ got the Secrets of the Ages tatted on our brains/ ways are so contagious/ same archaic phrases/ walking Hall of Ramses just going through the phases..." ~ Ozon from Space Suits EP

The Kemetic God, RA, is commonly described as the God of the Sun. RA is often equated with the life giving principles of the Rays of the Sun. RA (God of Creation), as in **Ra**diation, vibrates between positive and negative polarities which causes radiation to produce Particles such as protons, neutrons, electrons, and quarks etc. which come together to form Atoms (or Atum, God of Creation). From the radiation and interaction of particles (Atum) we get molecules, which in turn come together to form the various elements and states of matter here on Earth. These states of matter are the physical states of appearance perceived and experienced as a solid, liquid, gas, electricity, and space/vacuum. These states of matter which RA (radiation) and Atum (atoms) brought forth are personified in the divine personalities of the deities Geb (solid/earth), Tefnut (liquid/moisture), Shu (gas/air), Nut (space/vacuum), and Seker (electricity/energy)! From these states of matter we arrive at the organisms which embody the life of the planet. The organisms derived from the states of matter are manifested in stages of development from Minerals to Plants to Insects to Beasts/Animals to Man/Woman. The states of matter giving birth to organisms are reflected in the Creation Story as Geb, Tefnut, Shu, Nut, and Seker giving birth to Asar, Aset, Set, Nebethet, and Heru-Khuti! And from these organisms we get more organisms (ie. children, offspring, seeds, etc.), symbolized in the unification of Asar and Aset giving birth to Heru, the child with the spiritual warrior spirit, and chosen redeemer. Here, in the ancient Creation Story of Kemet, we can see a profound understanding of physics, biology, chemistry, the formulation of the varying states of matter and the manifestation of the material world. Our ancestors had a deep reverence for nature and cosmology and saw oneself as an integral and inseparable part of the Grand Reality we call God, Allah, The Source, The Creator, The All, etc. The story of Heru is a story of divine revelation, and the becoming of the true and living as a divine reflection and extension of the Great Spirit. Our way of life as a culture was designed to preserve our divinity, and manifest God in the physical world. Crystals and gemstones played an integral part in the elevation of our spiritual and natural energies and abilities, as well as anchoring the divine light here on the planet, and spreading that light along the planetary grid and ley lines. As the planet is composed of varying elements, with crystals within the earth at various points, the weight of the planet's surface which lays upon the crystals of earth, creates what is called piezoelectric and pyro-electric pulsations on and around the earth's surface. The effects of the piezoelectricity and pyro-electricity is what is responsible for generating the electromagnetic energy field which encompasses the Earth. Piezoelectricity is energy produced by pressure being exerted upon quartz crystals, where pyro-electricity is energy produced by the exertion of heat upon quartz crystals. In both instances, pyro-electricity and piezoelectricity, the energy generated and produced is quite beneficial and advantageous to the human electromagnetic energy circuitry. It is the balance of the electromagnetic energy of the human energy system which ensures and constitutes good health on all levels (mental, physical, emotional, and spiritual).

ENNEAD

ATUM / Ra
(Atom) (RAdiation)

CELESTIAL REALM
Hidden Unseen Realm
AMEN (0) The Creator

Celestial
"Cells"
Realm

Initial Source
Atomic Vibration

ELEMENTAL FORCES
COSMIC TERRESTRIAL REALM

1. SHU ~ OXYGEN
Hidden State
Air
Gas

2. TEFNUT ~ HYDROGEN
Unformed Matter State
Liquid/Moisture
Liquid/Water/Fire

Bio-Chemical LIFE

3. GEB ~ CARBON
Boundless State
Solid
Earth

4. NUT ~ NITROGEN
Dark State
Ether/Space/Nature
Sky

BiO-CHEMICAL LIFE
Protection and Proliferation of Nature/Neter

PHYSICAL REALM
Visible Seen Realm
ATUM (1)
Cosmic/Conceptual/
Human/Earth Realm

5. ASAR
Manifest
(throughout all nature)
Man
Elevation & Proliferation

6. ASET
Matter is Formed
Woman
Nurturer & Developer

7. SET
Bound & Configured
(into chemical properties)
Animals/Insects
Elevation & Proliferation

8. NEBT-HET
Light State
Plants/Minerals
Nurturer & Developer

Atomic Forces of Nature

MIND (0) ⇢ ATOMS (1) ⇢ ELEMENTS (2) ⇢ MINERALS (3) ⇢ PLANTS (4) ⇢ INSECTS (5) ⇢ ANIMALS (6) ⇢ HUMANS

Lesson 5

THE HUMAN BEING AS A LIGHT BODY

"I said, 'You are gods, And all of you are children of the Most High." Psalms 82:6

Emanating from each individual human being, and from collective groups of individuals, is an electromagnetic bio-photonic energy field capable of sending and receiving information on all levels. The human being can tune-in to the signals and frequencies of various energies being emanated from multiple planes within the immediate environment and/or great distances, be the energy of past, present, or future. The human organism can tune-in to the energetic frequencies via The Minds Eye's intuition, which is also known as the trifold combination of the brain, the pineal gland and the pituitary gland, which in turn stimulates the brains Alpha-Theta waves giving rise to the awareness level of the organism. The pineal gland and the opening of the 3rd Eye is stimulated by natural light and crystals! When light passes through a crystal the light gets fragmented into the various rays of the color spectrum, in turn assimilating the light-energy necessary for the stimulation of the individual's energy bodies and health balancing systems (i.e. chakras, meridians, etc.) to work towards optimum health and balance.

THE BASIC LEVELS OF THE HUMAN ENERGY BODIES

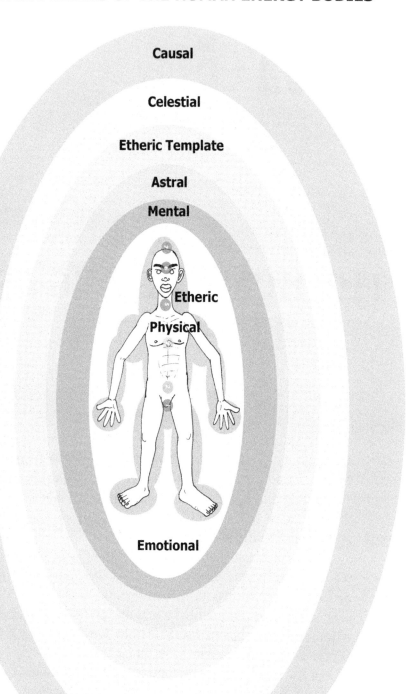

Causal

Celestial

Etheric Template

Astral

Mental

Etheric

Physical

Emotional

*The 7 Basic Chakras
on the Physical Body and just beyond.

In reality, all space is vibrating with sound and light energy. When observing the physical world we notice a wide-range of colors, each with varying degrees of tones and shades within each color of the spectrum. For example, there is a wide variety of varying shades of green in the green color ray of the color spectrum. However when observing the colors of "light" in contrast to the colors of "pigment" (animal/plant tissue), we begin to notice a few differences in the way in which color is expressed between Pigment and Light. Of primary distinction is the source from which each expression of color is produced. Contradictory to what many people think of in regards to light as being a 'bright-whitish gleam' is that the source of Light is actually Black! And Light, itself, goes NOWHERE! Light actually doesn't 'travel' anywhere at all. What actually happens with Light is that light always remains at its source, and (light) reflects (or radiates) at the speed rate of approximately 186,000 miles per second in normal atmospheric conditions. This means that Light itself is always at one with its source, and light is only reflected (or rather a reflection of the observer)...that reflection can be in the form of an object, a sound, a feeling, a thought, a touch, a memory, a being, the sun, ANYTHING! All we see is only a reflection of Light, constantly connected to and at one with the Source...when we recognize and align with this Source, our Source, forever present and emanating from the core of all things and beings, we begin to recognize the oneness that runs through, and is forever constant in, all things. Light teaches us the lessons of unity and the importance of literally radiating our light. Light itself has all the colors of the spectrum within it and it is only by slowing down the frequency, or by reflecting the light back without absorbing it, are we able to arrive at color in which we perceive. Light-colour initiates in darkness (black) and adds through the color spectrum towards white, while Pigment-colour (animals/plants etc.) initiate in darkness (black) and subtracts through the spectrum towards white. This science is highlighted in the creation story of the Bible which states *".., darkness was on the face of the deep...and God said 'Let there be light,' and there was light.."* What's actually happening when we're observing a colorful object is that light is being absorbed by the object, and the object simultaneously radiates (reflects) back the color (or colors) which have NOT been absorbed by the object. This means that what we see is really NOT what it is! For example, seeing two kids playing on a hot summer day with a big red bouncy ball, the big red ball is actually all the colors of the spectrum EXCEPT red, because all its true colors have been absorbed by the object (the ball), and only the color which has not been absorbed by the object has been reflected back to the atmosphere, which the average human eye perceives as the color red in this case. The colors of the things we see are not their true colors because the true colors of the objects we see are absorbed by the object. The wavelength of the radiation (emission) is what determines the color of light we perceive. This can be easily recognized by observing an object by day and then later observing that same object by night, and notice the differences in color grade.

In essence, and in all reality, all things are connected (in a non-local reality). All is One, and from the Oneness comes all things. On this physical plane, we experience and see the life of 'things' in duality (in example; hot and cold, darkness and light, unknown and known, male and female, positive and negative, etc.), however in reality, the duality is actually singular in essence, however expressed 3-dimensionaly in various shades or degrees (i.e. hot/cold, light/dark, liquid/solid etc.) on the spectrum (i.e. more/less etc.). All experiences are experienced from the perspective relative to the one (or each one individually) identifying the 'thing' being observed, rooted in ones previous experiences, likes and desires, as well as the circumstances and conditions of the current moment. The amazing reality of every experience is that while one (or group of individuals) is observing and/or experiencing a cipher (be it person, place or thing), the cipher (person, place, or thing) is simultaneously experiencing the one (or group of individuals) at the same time. There's a relay of energy exchange going on between the individual and the object (person, place or thing). As your atoms are inherently coded with intelligence, fixed locality (destination), choice, and your genetic make-up (DNA, etc.) and energy signature, so too are the molecules of other persons, places, and things. We notice this in various situations and circumstances in moments when we interact with someone, or walk into an environment, and we notice something about the energy of the person or environment etc. in which we are interacting. You may even be followed up with further thoughts of what may have taken place with the person or current location, and/or see visions or imprints of scenes, colors, smells, feelings, intuitive thoughts, and more in regards to the person, place or thing which you're interacting with. This is because the energy imprint is saturated there in that location. All is mental...All is Mind. Much of this is experienced because all things radiate light (streams of photons), known as molecular radiation, for all things are frozen light matter - light vibrating at a slower rate at which appears to be solid matter...however, nothing is truly solid but rather infinitesimal atoms coming together and vibrating at extremely fast rates (in relation to the human eyes ability of perception within the electromagnetic spectrum)! Every level of experience has its frequency of vibratory rate at which it is experienced and can be perceived.

(Exhibit C. Example of how energy fields interact within environments)

Lesson 6

MAN'S RESPONSE TO

VIBRATION

Man's Response To Vibration (in Vibrations Per Second)

Spiritual/Mental/Astral/Etheric......................Unknown
X-Ray...2 Trillion vps
Light Colour..500 Billion vps
Heat...200 Billion vps
Light..400,000 Million vps
Electricity...1,000 Million vps
Sound..16 – 32,768 vps
Solids..less than Sound

IMPORTANT NOTE:
Sound travels (*on a wave*) at approx. 1,120 feet/sec.
Light travels (*as a wave*) at approx. 186,000 miles/sec.

All Space is forever vibrating endlessly with Light and Sound. It is the humans' conscious awareness that picks-up on the vibrations already present that renders the experiences of feelings. Conscious awareness of the energy in the moment gives one a special feeling which is relative to the individual(s) experience in the moment... experienced as love, hate, anger, frustration, happiness, great joy, sadness, etc. These emotions (or energy in motion) are expressed as laughter, kisses, hugs, tears, fights, killing, giving birth, etc. Thus, good ideas, ideals, thoughts and the like give birth to good feelings, good vibrations, good experiences, and good outcomes overall. The thoughts you create and hold in your mind, shape and mold your reality and experiences. Everything you experience and that exists in your world now was once an existing thought you had in your mind and/or subconscious! All is Mind, and Mind manifests and expresses Itself through behavior (light and sound). Good ideas equates to good vibrations, good feelings, good actions, and good relations. Consequently, your thoughts control your vibrations, your ideas, and your feelings. We as humans have to be careful of this because We create our ideas and vibrations with our thoughts, however the Mind Itself manifests in All (including Humanity, Cosmos, etc.), All around, which means that if **our perception of thought** is NOT in alignment with That Which Is currently being observed and/or experienced we will be off (to whatever degree we misperceived) and we will have to face the repercussions of our thoughts and actions of mis-judgement. Therefore it would be wise to live out life with honor and respect for all life everywhere, and work and strive for preservation of Self in accordance with the beautiful virtues of Ma'at being Truth, Righteousness, Propriety (Respect), Harmony, Balance, Reciprocity (Equality), and Order. If we strive to live our lives filling our minds with rightful knowledge, and conducting ourselves wisely we will understand how much power we possess in our natural way of life, living in harmony and in balance with all things of Life, and beyond. It is through our Understanding, and respect, that we can be able to perceive our powerful connection with the Infinite Universal Source (ie. God, Great Spirit, Most High, Allah, etc.) within our own Being and all around, and our ability to create and manifest our thoughts finitely upon this plane in which we experience Life. All our lives and life experiences are, and will continue to be, based on our own thoughts and understanding. Everything you experience, and experienced, was once a thought you had. And that thought you had that created the experience along with the thought you had during and post the experiences gave birth to new and more thoughts... like a lotus flower. So we MUST tend the gardens of our minds regularly, keeping out negative thoughts which choke-out positive thoughts from manifesting, which often in turn renders poor experiences and low drives for more action. Keeping a positive Mind State initially can require great work, but once it becomes a habit, like everything else, it gets easier and easier to maintain, and more delightful and evident as you proceed and experience the results of your efforts.

Crystals are a great part of the work to be utilized by humanity to bring about balance upon the planet, however they are not necessarily the Absolute Answer to our development and inter-connectedness to each other, and/or Great Spirit. Though Crystals are marvelous in their appearance, amazing in their radiance, precise in technology, advantageous in science, beneficial in health, miraculous in mindfulness, and even much more yet untapped by modern society, Crystals are still tools of the Universe set here in place for Life to thrive upon, and live harmoniously in coexistence with. We as Humanity and Co-Creators of this world, and Nature as Animal, Insect, Plant, and Mineral Kingdoms, are all interconnected to one another and all things on multiple levels via Life Itself (existence/just being alive), for example people come together and usher influence through the use and/or awareness of genetics, language, mentality, ideology, consciousness, breath, biological composition, elemental structures, planetary influences, and gravitational pulls to name a few. All things coexist and work together in harmony, streaming and operating from whatever point on the spectrum they radiate from and/or originate within. All things are mental. All things are One.

Lesson 7

HOW IMPRINTING CRYSTALS OCCURS

"Allah is the Light of the heavens and the earth. The parable of His Light is as if there were a niche, And within it a lamp; the lamp enclosed in crystal, and the crystal shining as it were a brilliant star;" ~ Holy Qur'an 24:35

To understand how imprinting a crystal occurs between humanity and the mineral kingdom, there are a few basic scientific principles we need to be aware of which are at play in the process of imprinting. Those concepts include the Law of Conservation, the Law of Energy, the basic principles of the atom, and the basic principles of electromagnetism. Stated in the Law of Conservation is that the total mass present before a chemical reaction is the same as the total mass present after the chemical reaction (therefore the 'change/alteration' may not necessarily be noticed physically, but rather vibrational and/or subtle). The Law of Energy states that 'energy is neither created nor destroyed, but rather only transformed and/or transferred.'

As stated previously, energy can turn to matter and matter can turn into energy, all of which is structured and composed of atoms at its rudimentary level. All atoms, individually, inherently possess the full blueprint makeup of that which it composes. Therefore each atom of an object is already the seed, the tree, and the fruit...just going through the processes of growth and development. Each atom, individually, has inherent in its nature Intelligence, Choice, and a Destination which it is to reach, embody, and/or manifest. This ultimately translates to the individual atom having an Intelligent Consciousness, a Destination (or determined idea) it desires to reach and/or manifest, and also has Choice in the matter on how its going to 'get there'. This means that each individual atom is not only conscious, but also inherently holds the genetic makeup of the entire individual which it is a 'part' of.

Anything composed of atoms, naturally, has an electromagnetic quality to it, such as the physical body of humans, animals, insects, minerals, plants, etc. Electromagnetic energy is a from of energy which is reflected, or radiated, from an object in the form of electrical and magnetic waves that travel throughout space and time. Electromagnetic energy comes in the forms of Gamma Rays, X-Rays, Ultraviolet Radiation, Visible Light, Infrared Radiation, Microwaves, and Radio Waves... all of which together make up what is called the Electromagnetic Spectrum. Of the Electromagnetic Spectrum, Visible Light occupies but only an extremely minute portion of the spectrum; which lets us know that that which we perceive by way of our physical senses is but very little compared to what all is actually present and happening in our atmosphere on higher and lower frequencies within the spectrum. (see image below)

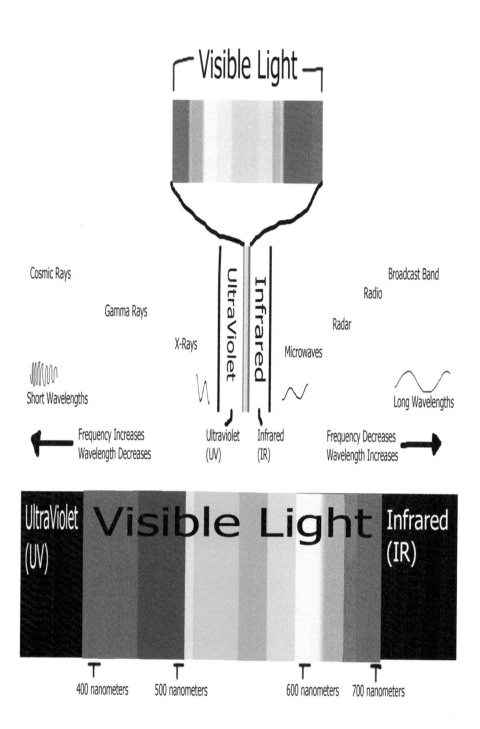

(Exhibit E. Electromagnetic Frequency Spectrum)

Electromagnetism is the interaction of electrical currents of Electricity and magnetic fields of Magnetism. Electricity is the projective Yang energy quality that results from the existence of charged particles (ie protons, electrons, etc.), while Magnetism is defined as the receptive Yin energy quality and the attractive/repulsive forces at work resulting from the motion of an electrically charged object or objects. The magnetism is generated by the orbiting of electrons within the atoms of an object or substance. Magnetic fields can be generated by aligning atoms, which one can do by way of mental projection and/or energy channeling and focusing ones intent. Both, Magnetism and Electricity, are necessary to balance the individual being and sustain life on the physical plane...the brain (mental plane) and body (physical plane) being electrical by nature and composition, and the emotion (emotional plane) and spirit (spiritual plane) being magnetic by nature and composition. Evidence of this can be easily experienced in the phenomenon of Love and the 'attractive powers' (magnetism) one feels towards the object of ones affection, in contrast to the 'electrical' feeling one experiences when touching and kissing a loved one. Both electricity and magnetism help to create and complete the bond, as well as assist in forming the connection, between the individuals in the interaction. What is resulted is the releasing of special endorphins, which in turn create an intense euphoric feeling in the positive initial 'spark' of what we call love! However, this same principle is at work when two opposing forces or objects interact. When two opposing forces interact, instead of the interaction producing an attractive quality, this time it will produce a repulsive quality, driving the two opposing forces or objects further apart, or to a point of overstimulation. What is resulted from the opposing forces interaction is often a negative energetic residue, which if not balanced or cleared can bring about dis-ease and dis-comfort, and sometimes... great disaster. So as we can see here, when it comes to the mixing and intermingling of energies and forces, it is of utmost importance and would be quite wise to be aware of the energy it is that we possess and are projecting, at the same time be aware of the energy that is best or most conducive for us to be around, as well what is the energy of the atmosphere in which we currently are residing in...and is it conducive to our own growth and development and expression of our truth. If the answer is NO or negative on any of these accounts, then changes need to be made that will be most favorable and suitable to ones optimal growth and development and expression of Self. One way one can influence the energy of the current environment and atmosphere is by utilizing crystals, and imprinting crystals with the energy most conducive to ones growth and development and expression of truth. One way one can use crystals to influence their environment is by imprinting crystals with positive energy, and incorporating crystals that counter negativity and harmful radiation (such as Rose Quartz, Selenite, Black Tourmaline, Watermelon Tourmaline, Shungite, etc.). One can program such crystals with the intentions necessary to assist one in radiating their energy (emotions, thoughts, creativity, etc.) at levels they are comfortable with, even to new heights previously unexplored. Crystals can be programmed through a process called *Imprinting.*

The way imprinting occurs in the object being programmed is by way of its atomic structure. All things with an atomic structure has an electromagnetic quality to it which has the ability to be programmed and/or encoded or imprinted with your own personal 'energy signature' vibration, and your specific intent for which you intend the 'thing' to be used at its energetic core level, or what you want it to assist you in manifesting...in this case the object we are talking about imprinting is the crystal. Now of the human beings physical composition, the largest organ of the human body is the human skin! Crystals, at the molecular level, have a similar crystalline structure that resembles that of human beings. Just as every individual human being gives off and absorbs electromagnetic energy, so do crystals – which I will explain shortly. The skin being the largest organ of the physical biological system, when a human being touches a crystal, be it "yours" or not, the human being imprints the crystal with their energy signature, and if they focus their intention with the crystal in hand they can imprint the crystal with their intention(s)...which may not always be good. Therefore, it is always a good practice to clear, cleanse, and charge each and every crystal you acquire, and if you can do it regularly with the full and/or new moon cycles even better! *To keep your crystal clear, charged, and programmed see the corresponding section.*

As stated earlier, each crystal has its own energetic signature and intent, which in turn has influence upon the surroundings, objects and/or beings within its environment and beyond as well. Much of the energy signature at the energetic core level of a person, place, or thing will already be predetermined as we learned earlier, in which all atoms have a destiny and/or determined idea (a.k.a. Purpose) for which it is existing and exercising. The more an energy influence is nurtured and projected the more it begins to mix into the energy signature, which in turn begins to quicken the process of manifestation and increase the influence of probabilities of manifesting your visions upon the physical plane. This means, by interacting with or keeping crystals within your environment working intentionally towards a specific desired goal or outcome beneficial to the greatest good of all concerned, the energies of the crystals project prominence toward the greatest universal outcome...which may sometimes be beyond our understanding. However, by understanding that the energy of Space through which we move and exist is also full of these atoms which are in a constant state of vibrational flux, we can begin to see how all things and all space is in constant vibration...and the only things truly separating one thing from another is ultimately the vibrational frequency rate at which things vibrate. A tree vibrates at the rate of the tree and is composed of the atoms that are coded with that specific (group and individual) tree's essences (all that the tree is/was/will be), while a fish vibrates at its frequency and is composed of its atoms, and so goes it for all things on all frequencies of the spectrum...each having its Group Frequency and Composition, as well its own individual vibration within that frequency which renders it its own specific 'energy signature' or vibratory rate (its own unique energy).

Atoms are composed of Protons, Neutrons, and Electrons, all of which stay constantly in motion. The Protons being of a positive electrical charge are equal in magnitude to the Electrons. Electrons carry a negative electrical charge and possess a magnetic energy which interacts with the protons of the object to create Electromagnetic energy fields. These subtle electromagnetic energy fields of objects give off energy that interacts with other electromagnetic energy within the Electromagnetic Energy Spectrum. The human being generates a quite powerful electromagnetic energy field.   Humans are constantly radiating (electrical) and absorbing (magnetic) energy of various types of wavelengths and frequencies known as *blackbody radiation*.   A blackbody is an organism/body or an object that absorbs all the electromagnetic radiation, or in other words forms of light, that touches it. In order for the body to stay in thermal stability the blackbody must emit radiation at the same rate it absorbs it. This symmetric state of vibration makes the blackbody not only the optimal absorber but also the ideal radiator as well. Blackbody radiation is the energy a physical body/object absorbs (takes in) and radiates (gives off) in relation to its environment and surroundings at every given moment. This translates to meaning that the human being interacts with its environment and surroundings, at every level, at all times. Therefore, the human being is constantly communicating and interacting, sending and absorbing signals and messages, leaving imprints on and absorbing energy from any and every person, thing, and place we've been, touched, passed through, interacted with, didn't interact with; the human being is interacting with all things electromagnetically, on frequencies beyond the visible spectrum within the electromagnetic spectrum!

Blackbody radiation is a key element in determining ones energy signature pattern. In other words, the frequency rate at which one vibrates becomes a part of ones energy signature. Other elements include ones spiritual energy body and will power, ones physical body, ones mental energy, ones emotional energy, along with ones lifetimes of experience and memory... most of which residing outside the visible physical spectrum; similar to the storing of information from your physical iPhone or computer to the memory of the universal iCloud, each one (user) having their own password to tap into their personal email, as well as Google universal information! The human being is an amazing existence and the body is a profound, yet fragile, machine! It is no wonder why the many of our breakthrough creations have been modeled based on the mechanics of the human body (i.e. Camera = Eye, Microphone = Ear, Computer = Brain, etc.). Do you see now why it is important to clear and program your crystal, and center and balance your mind and body?

Lesson 8

ON KEEPING CRYSTALS

"Moreover, I will make your battlements of rubies, and your gates of crystal, and your entire wall of precious stones."
~ Isaiah 54:12

Crystals have been around for over thousands of years, some since the early stages of the Earth's formation. Some form by way of seeding (a form of planting crystals, like planting seeds), some form by way of mixing (or breeding) with other minerals in the crystal kingdom, while still others arrive by way of intergalactic contact (meteorites and/or space debris). With such a long history of existence on our planet, and throughout our galaxy, crystals have experienced a wide range of Earth changes in all it's forms and phases. Through weathering the phases of these periods, crystal have grown and manifested the ability to render their own experience and knowledge to their keepers in the form of electrical impulses presented to the mind in the form of intuition, inspiration, and /or euphoric sensations, as well as providing a protective shield against positive ions and radiation detrimental to the human body and structure.

Crystals, like human beings, pick up all types of energy throughout the day, months, and over the years. Like humans, when crystals have accumulated too much energy without being cleared and/or cleansed, they will begin to lower in vibrancy and look deficient in luster. Like a fatigued basketball player playing long stints of time being unable to perform at their optimum level, so too is the crystal when not regularly cleansed and charged! They become almost lackluster. I say 'almost' but not quite because they are still crystals, and being that they are crystals they will remain true to their essence in spite all odds... Intensity may vary and programming may change, but the crystal will always remain true to its essence...a gift acquired over their years of evolution and endurance. To properly get the most out of your crystals, I have listed here are a few suggestions to follow to be sure your crystals maintain their brilliance and programming throughout your duration with them.

As stated previously, crystals accumulate energy throughout their time traveling... long before they get to you [remember, crystals are thousands of years old, some even millions]. One of the first things you will want to do when you first acquire a crystal is clear the crystal of any previous energy or programming which may not be beneficial nor useful to you. Remember, many of these crystals come from deep within the Earth and have been mined out (in various ways, under various conditions) and have been transported (in a variety of ways) with a variety of different intentions passing through their crystalline structures while in the hands (and/or atmospheres) of their carriers and possessors. You never know who was with it before you...remember, crystals are thousands of years old, some even millions!

HOW TO CLEAR A CRYSTAL (of previous energy and programming)

1. **SMUDGE** – Burn Sage, and blow Sage smoke on and all over the crystal for several minutes (10mins+).

2. **INTENTION** – While Smudging the crystal send your thought (Mind Intention) into the center of the crystal, a thought of *"Clearing the Crystal of All Negative Energy, and Aligning the Crystal with The Greatest Good Of All Concerned"*. You can perform this with the crystal in your hand (programming hand, or both hands sending energy from palm chakras into the crystal).

3. (If Available) **SINGING BOWL** - Chime Chimes and/or play Singing Bowl, directing (through intention) the healing energy of the sounds towards the crystal… Remember, *'Energy Follows Intent'*. You can let Sage burn near crystal while playing/chiming singing bowl or chimes.

The whole Clearing Crystal Process will take anywhere from 10-20 minutes or more depending on how much time you allow, as well as what your intuition guides you to do. Throughout the process one is to bear a positive and loving energy and intention to assure one is using the crystal in the correct capacity.

I caution you all here::: Using Crystals for other than good, or for ones own avarice and/or savagery in the pursuit of self-gratification can be Dangerous! Do NOT tamper with the essence of the crystals and attempt to use them for negativity, for it can be detrimental to your own self.

Use crystals honorably and in a good spirit and with a good mind, and with good intentions. Incorporating crystals into your lifestyle and healing therapies will add many benefits. Crystals are to be added to one's healing, not to necessarily replace the current treatment and healing methods.

Lesson 9

HOW TO PROGRAM A CRYSTAL

Programming a crystal is the process of projecting your personal intention into a crystal and saturating that crystal with your own personal intentions and energy signature. You can program a crystal with your own personal intentions through channeling (or collecting/gathering/focusing) your energy (from within and around your being), and focusing your thought-intention energy and sending it to (into the center of) the crystal. Energy follows intent. **ENERGY FOLLOWS INTENTION.** Therefore, one must conduct oneself responsibly, and in accordance with the greatest good of all concerned. That said, be aware that Crystals are of the Mineral Kingdom. The Mineral Kingdom is of the Planet's formation; making the Mineral Kingdom the organs of the Planets. The Minerals, being the elements of which the Human Kingdom is composed, gives the Human Kingdom a direct connection and relation with the Mineral Kingdom. It is like the Human Kingdoms' relation to the Plant, Insect, Animal, Celestial, Astro (Planets, Suns, Stars, etc.), Astral, and Spiritual Kingdoms. All is connected to all in the All-In-All. Therefore, humanity should go forth with solicitude toward one another, and conduct oneself with respect and appreciation toward the Natural World in which we live. Therefore, when programming a Crystal, and working with a Crystal in general, work with good intentions for the greater good of all concerned (involved and/or related).

Programming a crystal is quiet simple. The main principle to remember and keep in mind here is that "Energy follows intent". Wherever it is you consciously direct your intention is the direction in which your energy flows. An example in which we see can this principle in action is when a person may have done something which appeared to be ill (negative) with a good intention at heart, and another may have done something which appears to be quite good with a self-centered intention held in mind. For example, in an act of self-preservation and the continuation of family legacy one may have killed another being whom posed immediate harm and danger to ones family. On the other hand, another person may have given a homeless person a few dollars only to look good in front of others and later to write it off in taxes and get his money back in a tax return. In both examples, the GREATEST GOOD OF ALL CONCERNED was served in the universal scheme of things: The family's legacy will continue to live on and the immediate danger to the lineage was removed in the first example, and in the second example, the homeless was provided for in the moment while the greedy one, whom was the provider, maybe not even have been aware of the fact he was serving a greater cause, and if he was aware possibly not to the extent in which he served... thus making both incidents serving the greatest good of all concerned. But what happens when evil thrives over good through the use of evil acts... Such as in war? In such cases EVERYONE suffers. There are no victories in battles where innocent lives are lost... for every life is valuable and important and there is NONE other like it! Therefore we must begin establishing new relationships with each other, and our surroundings. For as we breathe and marvel at life on Earth and the cosmos all around, so does our Great Mother Earth! Therefore we must be conscious and cautious as to where we direct our attention, and channel our energy for positive production upon this physical plane. As all starts within the mind, and we must cultivate our minds with thoughts of positivity and constructive change and development, to re-create the world in which we desire to live. We can utilize Crystals to assist in channeling such energy, and grounding it into the Earth's Celestial Grid, which in turn harmonizes the Earth's energy, stabilizes ours, and brings both into resonance with one another to be elevated to higher frequencies in unison.

Lesson 10

ASTROLOGICS: COSMOLOGY AND HUMANITY

"I said, Ye are gods; and all of you are children of the Most High. But ye shall die like men, and fall like one for the princes. Arise, O God, judge the earth: for thou shalt inherit all nations."
~Psalm 82:6-8

There are many ancient scriptures that relate the cosmos to humanity, and linking humanity to the cosmos. There are many reflecting patterns and rhythms found in nature and throughout the cosmos that reflect the nature of humanity and life on earth. By understanding our human nature and our natural cycles, we can begin to get a better understanding of what's going on around us in the cosmos, as well as within our environment, and also internally at the atomic and molecular levels within our own selves. All is a reflection of the All...or as one of the Universal Principle's states, "As above, so below". Humanity is only a microcosm of the macrocosm called the Universe and/or God.

Therefore, Humanity is the Micro-Organism and the Universe/God is the Macro-Organism, each one reflecting and resembling the similar patterns and rhythms of the other.

To get a closer look at the relationship of the macro-micro reflection of the cosmos and humanity we must first have a basic understanding of solar and planetary movement and Astrological Ages, which describes how planets tailspin-orbit around the sun as the sun cycles its way throughout the Ecliptic also known as the Celestial Sphere, the Zodiacal Constellations, and also the Milky Way Galaxy. It is important to note here that officially there are approx. 88 Constellations, however, our solar system passes through approx. 13 of them, yet 12 are considered the official Signs of the Zodiac. The 13th Sign is Ophiuchus, the Age of the Serpent Bearer, which occupies the heavens between approx. November 29th to December 17th. However, Ophiuchus, occupying a space in the heavens for such a short period of time many astrologic systems discount Ophiuchus as a Sign to be considered when analyzing the Zodiac Chart.

*1 AGE = 2,160 - 2,166 years

WINTER SOLSTICE
(Sun at Lowest Point)

WEST GATE - WESTERN HEMISPHERE

WINTER SOLSTICE

SPRING EQUINOX
(Sun Rise / Sun at Equal Day & Night)

FALL EQUINOX

SOUTH GATE - EASTERN HEMISPHERE

EASTERN HEMISPHERE - EAST GATE

NORTH GATE - WESTERN HEMISPHERE

- CAPRICORN (GOAT)
CARDINAL - Getting Things Started
"I Use"
EARTH - SATURN - CAREER
- SOCIAL STATUS
12/21 - 1/21

+ AQUARIUS (WATER BEARER)
FIXED
"I Know"
AIR - SATURN - URANUS
- FRIENDS - HOPES
1/21 - 2/21

+ SAGITTARIUS (ARCHER)
MUTABLE - Changeable & Varying
"I See/Aspire Higher"
FIRE - JUPITER - ASPIRING
- LEARNING

OPHIUCHUS (SERPENT BEARER)
11/22 - 12/22

OPHIUCHUS (SERPENT BEARER)
11/30 - 12/17

- SCORPIO (SCORPION)
FIXED
"I Desire"
WATER - PLUTO - MARS -
EXITS - LEGACY
10/23 - 11/22

- PISCES (FISH)
MUTABLE - Changeable and Varying
"I Believe"
WATER - NEPTUNE - JUPITER -
SPIRITUAL CONFIRMATION
2/21 - 3/21

+ LIBRA (BALANCE SCALE)
CARDINAL - Getting Things Started
"I Unite/Balance"
AIR - VENUS - BLOOD -
UNITY - FAMILY
9/23 - 10/23

Relationships 11
Wealth 10
LIFE 9
Endings 8
Relationships 7
Endings 12
Wealth 1
LIFE 2
Wealth 6
Endings 4
LIFE 5
Relationships 3

+ ARIES (RAM)
CARDINAL - Getting Things Started
"I Am"
FIRE- MARS - ENERGY
3/21 - 4/21

- VIRGO (VIRGIN)
MUTABLE - Changeable & Varying
"I Analyze"
EARTH - MERCURY -
EMPLOYMENT - HEALTH
8/23 - 9/23

- TAURUS (BULL)
FIXED
"I Have"
EARTH - VENUS -
PERSONAL PROSPERITY
4/21 - 5/21

+ LEO (LION)
FIXED
"I Will/Create"
FIRE - SUN - CREATIVITY
- OFFSPRING
7/22 - 8/22

+ GEMINI (TWINS)
MUTABLE - Changeable & Varying
"I Think"
AIR -MERCURY -
RELATIVES &
NEIGHBORS/COMMUNITY
5/21 - 6/21

- CANCER (CRAB)
CARDINAL - Getting Things Started
"I Feel"
WATER - MOON - LATER YEARS
6/21 - 7/21

SUMMER SOLSTICE
(Sun at Highest Point)

Solar and Planetary Movement Measurements:

"Then God said, 'Let there be lights in the firmament of the heaven to divide the day from the night; and let them be for signs and for seasons and for days and years" ~ Genesis 1:14

1 DAY = 1 Complete rotation (spin) of the Earth.
- Measures the Earth's spin (rotation) as it travels (tail-spins) around the Sun.
- Approx. 24 hours

1 MONTH = 1 Complete revolution (circling) of the Moon around the Earth.
- Measures the movement of the Moon as it orbits (circles) around the Earth.
- Approx. 30 Days (720 hours)

1 YEAR = 1 Complete revolution of the Earth circling (tail-spinning) around the Sun.
- Measures the Earth's movement around (or in relation to) the Sun as the Sun and Earth orbit throughout the Solar System.
- Approx. 365 (or 366 Leap Year) Days (8,760/8,784 hours)

1 (ASTROLOGICAL) AGE = 1 Complete movement of the Sun through 1 Zodiacal Constellation (ie. the Sun moving through Pisces before entering Aquarius).
- Measures the movement of the Sun and Earth (Solar System) through an Astrological Age (part of the Galaxy).
- 1 Age is approx. 30 Degrees
- Every 72 years we move 1 degree through an Age
- 1 Age is approx. 2,160 (to 2,166) years

1 SOLAR CYCLE (Precession of the Equinoxes) = 1 Complete cycle of the Sun and Earth through All of the Astrological Ages as they (Sun/Earth) move through the Galaxy.
- Measures the movement of the Sun and Earth (Solar System) throughout the entire Ecliptic (Galaxy/Celestial Sphere)
- **Approx. 25,920 years!!**

AVERAGE HUMAN BREATHING MEASUREMENTS:

"The Spirit of God has made me, and the breath of the Almighty gives me life." ~ Job 33:4

On average the Human Being breathes...

1 DAY = 18 Breaths per Minute

18 Breaths per Minute = 72 Pulses per Minute!

18 Breaths per Minute = 25,920 Breaths per Day!!!

KEY POINTS:::

- 25,920 Breaths per Day SAME AS 25,920 years to 1 complete Solar Cycle!

- 72 Pulses per Minute REFLECTING the 72 Degrees of separation on the human being (between the arm, leg, leg, arm, and head stretched out)!

360 Degrees of Woman and Man
5 x 72* Degrees of Separation = 360*
Arm, Leg, Leg, Arm, Head (A.L.L.A.H.)

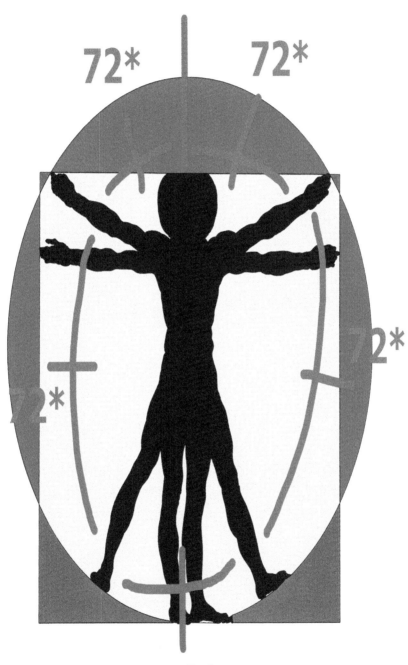

Lesson 11

BRAINWAVE ACTIVITY & BREATH CONTROL: KEYS TO YOUR INNER PORTALS

"Allah takes the souls at the time of their death, and those that do not die [He takes] during their sleep. Then He keeps those for which He has decreed death and releases the others [to their bodies] for an appointed term. Indeed in that are signs for a people who give thought." ~ Holy Qur'an 39:42

The human brain is the receptor and processor of the external signals the body receives by means of the 5 physical senses of Sight, Sound, Taste, Smell, and Touch. Each part of the body has its organs of perception which help to receive signal from the outside world. Each organ of reception (i.e. eyes, ears, nose, tongue, and hand) has thousands of receptors responsible for sending specific information to the brain for further analysis and organization. For example, the human being has a total of 10,000 taste buds, 9,000 found on the tongue, and another 1,000 found on the cheeks and palate of the mouth, responsible for relaying signals for how things taste. The brain then takes this information and organizes it, running by the mind (be it sleep or awakened) and emotions, determining how it "feels" about what it experienced (i.e. sweet, cold, enjoyable, etc.), and then it connects the experience to a previous (or similar) experience, filing it all away for later. Many of the files in the human memory are accessed by use of the brain, however it is critical to mention that much of the human memory and experiences are registered in the DNA genetic code, much of which has been deluded as "junk DNA". There is a misnomer which states that over 95% of the human DNA is so-called useless and unproductive and is mislabeled "junk DNA". As the tale of genetic evolution exposes, whatever is useless to the genetic structure and development for survival gets evolved out within a few generations. There is no such thing as "junk DNA". That which has been inaccurately labeled as "junk DNA" is a misnomer contributed by Dr. Susumu Ohno in a 1972 article called "So Much 'Junk DNA", and the term swiftly fastened to the scientific community, and has stuck with it since. The human being has within this so-called "junk DNA" *pseudo genes,* which ultimately are fossils of older (could be ancient) genes which remain within the coding, but however for whatever reason remain asleep, or inactive. There are ways to activate the inactive strands of your DNA by way of meditations, breathing, focused visualizations, sounds, herbs, martial arts, yoga, and other various practices and rituals. The ancient coding can be reawakened by means of ancient practices of mindfulness, health and healing, martial arts, breath control, crystal integration (incorporating crystals in your lifestyles and healing practices) and various other means of self-actualization. Humanity, at this time of this writing, is a sleeping giant!

Back to the human brain and the senses...

Now you can add a 6th sense to the Human element, being that of Intuition. Intuition is defined as "the ability to understand something immediately, without the need for conscious reasoning; a thing that one knows of considers likely from instinctive feeling rather than conscious reasoning." Intuition is the ability to pick-up on the energy operating presently in motion. With further practice, one can strengthen ones intuition and begin to discern what the energy is, and/or is saying, the message and/or lesson of the energy, and sometimes even where the energy initiated, and what its purpose is in your life. The purpose of the energy, be the energy a person, place, or thing, is all about what its role takes on in your life. It is often found to be something of a beneficial nature, guiding one to peace, safety, healing, guidance, love, harmony, self, abundance, and other positive things, or signs of warning and/or caution. Intuition can be further segmented into various forms of intuition, such as clairvoyance, clairsentience, clairaudience, claircognizance, and clairalience.

Clairvoyance is defined as the ability to perceive events in the future, present, and/or past, or beyond normal sensory contact.

Clairsentience is defined as the ability to feel the present, past or future physical and emotional states of others, without the use of the normal five senses; the ability to intuitively retrieve information from people, places, and things.

Clairaudience is defined as the ability to hear and/or perceive sounds or words from outside sources not audible to the normal ear; often heard internally via intuition or mentally, and/or within the ears.

Claircognizance is defined as the ability to intuitively know something to be true without supporting knowledge, logic, reason, and/or even awareness of knowing that one "knew"; the ability to retrieve knowledge and/or information intuitively.

Clairalience is defined as the ability to retrieve specific information intuitively through the use of the scent of smell.

With all these responsibilities under the management of the brain, it is the duty of each of the senses to report back, constantly, to the brain, which then is stimulated in various way, triggering various chemical reactions susceptible to all the physical and higher bodies. The images, sounds, impressions, and all the actions and emotions then get filed in the DNA and the brains memory bank, as well as recorded in the Universal Conscious Mind (or Universal Consciousness) in what is commonly known as the Akashic Records, for later retrieval and reflection, as well as for the present moment for thinking and communicating (i.e. having a conversation with a friend about a historical event). The Akashic Records is a fourth dimensional etheric field of high vibrational frequency which holds the impressions of every thought, word, action, and feeling ever to have been thought and/or experienced in this lifetime, and all others...likened to the Super Conscious Mind. This fourth dimensional field of impressionable recording not only contains the memory of the thoughts and experiences, but also allows the human being to tap into the frequency and gain access to the information, at any time, when ones mind and being has been properly attuned, and prepared to enter such states of consciousness.

To gain access to such powerful information is not just given to anyone, and is something not to be taken lightly either, nor used in any negative type of way. To gain access to such information is not so easily accessible, for one has to be dedicated and put in much work and effort in the pursuit of awakening the Higher Self. Awakening the Higher Self, one will be able to walk the Earth as a true reflection of Creator, Source Energy, Light, Love, God, Allah, Jah, Amen, Ra, Asar, Heru, etc. By anchoring the Light within ones self, and manifesting that Light on this third dimensional field, one walks the earth a true and living god; notice how I used the lower-case "g" to symbolize humanity as the micro-reflection, congruous to the Source/God with the capital "G" to symbolize the macro-universal supreme All in All. This is because humanity and the Source are ALWAYS connected...AT THE SOURCE...just like light. WHY??? Because EVERYTHING IS fragmented LIGHT!!! The palpable universe we perceive and experience with our physical beings and intangible minds is truthfully (to the fullest degree) a projection of light...a third dimensional depiction generated by light beams of consciousness...a conscious hologram!

The brain is composed of billions and billions of microscopic cells called neurons, which communicate by way of sending electrical, or chemical, signals to each other through organic structures in the brain called synapses. The brain is vitally influenced by the breath and the heart, which are responsible for pumping oxygen and sustenance to the brain to maintain its functions, as well as opening doorways within the mind to higher learning and access to higher realms of being and information, as you will see. The human body is of electromagnetic composition, and produces immense amounts of electrical activity within the brain, and through the use of precise electrical measuring medical equipment, scientists can measure the levels of activity, or rate at which electrical activity is occurring, within the brain. Over courses of studies, scientists have been able to section and label the general activities and functioning of the brain at the various frequencies observed. Below is a chart, which very briefly highlights the brainwave activity frequencies, their basic modes of operation, as well the ranges between which they kick-in and function. Brainwave activity, here, is measured in electrical pulses per second (pps).

BRAINWAVE ACTIVITY CHART

(Measured in Electrical Pulses Per Second)

BRAINWAVE STATE	ACTIVITIES	Pulses Per Second
GAMMA	Functions in response to intense emotions +/-.	29-35 pps
BETA	Normal waking state.	13-28 pps
ALPHA	Daydreaming, Light Meditational, Now-ness.	8-12 pps
THETA	Deep Meditation, Dream, REM, Vivid Visions.	3-7 pps

DELTA   REM, Full Sleep, Dreamless, Deepest Meditation. 5-3 pps

Now, to connect the dots, we must start with looking at the average human being, carrying on with life at their regular average state. On average, at the normal waking state, the Beta State, the human being breathes 18 breaths per minute and the heart pulsates blood through the system at 72 pulses per minute; which reflects the 72 degrees between each limb of the human composition – arm, leg, leg, arm, and head. Breathing 18 breaths per minute, at the average normal waking state, in turn equates to 25,920 breaths per day; which also reflects the pattern of the cosmos, being that of 25,920 years to 1 complete precession of the equinox, reflecting our divine direct connection to the Source of All Creation. We are truly One with the Universe, and simultaneously a reflection of it! Now as we experience this universe our experiences are experienced by ourselves, as well as that which we are experiencing be it a person, place, or thing. So we see there is a constant interconnectedness and interaction going on at ALL times. As we send signals (energy frequencies, photons, light, etc.) of electromagnetic radiation, we receive them as well. All energy signals coming to the human body are not necessarily all good for the human organism. Some of the energies penetrating the human system are quite damaging, and in some cases, vital. These signals, often in the form of positive ions (harmful to the human system) and negative ions (beneficial to the human system) can be found in various locations all over the planet and throughout the cosmos. In general, you will find an abundance of positive ions (harmful radiation) around big cities, computer technology, cars and trains, heavy smoke, grafted sounds, etc. while you will find an abundance of negative ions (beneficial radiation) around waterfalls, nature, plants, trees, natural life living freely, oceans, streams, forests, natural environments and atmospheres of love and peace and enjoyment being expressed. These negative ions can be stimulated to generate intense euphoric emotions (Gamma Waves) within an individual experiencing such environments. These signals we are sending and receiving are coded with information which can be picked-up on, or tuned-in to, to gain a better understanding of the energy currently operating, or presently in motion, to improve circumstances and/or situations for a greater outcome and/or good for all concerned. But just like those intensely positive emotions can stimulate and program the beautiful in response to stimulated emotions, so too can the intensely negative emotions be stimulated and programmed with extremely ugly responses to negative and/or fearful situations or emotions. The Gamma Wave frequency is where the activities of the brain respond and react to the internal and external environment, based on what has been programmed previously (in this life experience or previous lifetimes) by the Alpha and Theta states of brainwave activity. The Gamma Wave frequency kicks-in in response to ones thoughts, emotions, and/or fears.

Now as we relax and recline into our relaxation mind, the body and the breath begins to slow down. And quite concurrently, as the breath slows down so too does the body and mind. So one could truly begin with what comes easiest to focus on, breath (breath control) or thoughts (affirmations, mantras, mandalas), to begin the process of slowing down the body and mind, placing them all (mind, body, and breath) into a light meditative, day-dreamy type of state, called the Alpha State. The Alpha State is a that state just before you go to sleep or right when you wake up in the morning. Now personally for me, that is my FAVORITE part of the day...waking up! There's a newness and an excitement that takes place when I open my eyes for the first time in the morning that feels almost magical. Almost like an "I can't believe its real"...like when I'm waking up, I'm actually waking up IN a lucid dream (as opposed to going asleep into the Dreamworld). The more and more I'm on this Earth, the more I feel we have many of the roles and concepts we hold reversed...one being the Dreamworld being the dream, and the waking world being the "real world"...when its quite REAL that we cannot carry on without returning to the "dream" world...and someday, when we exit the Grand Stage of Life, we exit like a going to sleep...a long sleep...so deep some of whom in waking life have still yet to awaken. However, at this Alpha State, the mind is awake but still rather relaxed, centered, and unveiling. The Alpha State is the supreme state for self-programming transformations within self and impressing visions upon the conscious, and sub-conscious, mind to carry out and respond with when the Gamma Waves are stimulated. The Alpha State is ideal for intentionally programming self with desired responses one would like to integrate in ones life. It is often from a repetitive cycle of 21 consecutive days to lock a pattern, response, or habit within the human psyche, which then becomes habit and/or second nature. Just as habits and programs can be imprinted, they can be overridden and/or reprogrammed by the Self as well (be it at a conscious, sub-conscious or super-conscious level). This is where the science behind meditation, affirmations and mantras, and the process of repetition holds key elements to our expansion and understanding of Self. Through the use of applying proper breathing, proper thinking, proper action, proper intention, proper words, proper lifestyle, proper emotions and proper diet we can begin to access even greater depths of awareness and understanding of Self, Creation, nature of Source Energy, and much much more. This is where we also notice the powerful design of the 8-Fold Path towards Enlightenment, which the Buddha so lovely spoke about in his first teachings of the Four Noble Truths. The Four Nobel Truths lead one to look beyond the appearance of things, into the root of the causes and rise above by realizing and actualizing your power by way of taking self control over all aspects of ones life, rending ones life and lifestyle to the service of the greatest good of all concerned...contributing positive energy to the whole of humanity...anchoring their Light to the physical world, showing and proving the reality and love of Source Energy expressed though their way of life. So now we see that the Alpha State is the key to opening that first doorway into the deeper portals of Self. As noted before, as the breath slows down the mind sinks deeper and deeper and deeper into the abyss of the Consciousness...so we see that the body and breath is the "boat and paddles" we use to ride the waves of Consciousness! Heaven and Earth come together in the physical form of man and woman, with all its abilities and possibilities. Earth (body), Air (breath), Fire (Spirit), Water (emotions/wisdom) all come-together in the apex of the physical living human being. If only we all knew who we were, and our magnificent powers which lay actively latent within our composition, imagine the astronomical scale of life we would be existing as... Sleeping giants.

As the breath slows more, we steep a little further into the deep meditative states, or sleep, which swing open the doors to higher learning, dreaming (associated with rapid eye movement – REM), a greater understanding of life on multiple spheres and of inter-dimensional origins, the ability to access information previously unavailable to the conscious waking mind, and more. In the Theta State, the mind is in an extremely relaxed state. The Mind, in the Theta State, is very susceptible to hypnosis, by self or others, and accessing information from the sub-conscious mind through a series of questions and answers, or visionary experiences. The Theta State, being associated with deep meditation, provides access to the higher dimensions of existence and reality of Self, allowing access to the ability to travel energetically, also known as Astral Projection and/or Astral Travel. In this Theta State, the breath count per minute is slow and rhythmic, our physical senses are inhibited to the outside world but very lively in tune with the internal universe happening within Self. Vivid dreams and lucid imagery occur in this Theta State, which have proven to hold, and provide, profound breakthroughs not only for individuals, but also communities, industries, species, land, and the planet as a whole. Dreams often provide profound information, and/or insight, about specific topics, issues, and situations in which the spirit is prepared to currently address, and/or about to occur, or energies currently in motion that the individual should be consciously privy to. It is by actualizing the breakthroughs we experience internally in such dreams and trances, and manifesting them in this physical plane, is where we begin to see the brilliant creations flowering from creative minds, whom modern day society have deemed "genius"; however in all reality, we all have genius in us...most of us just have yet to realize our own uniqueness, and actualize our genius gifts. At the Theta State, one can begin to access past-life experiences and energy (karma) carried over to be worked out this lifetime, often known as Soul Contracts. Soul Contracts are contracts agreed upon by you, and other spirit beings (energies), at a spiritual/energetic level prior to conception, to make manifest and carry out on this physical third dimensional plane during and after conception.

The Delta frequency is the next vibratory state of brainwave activity. At the Delta State, the body is fully asleep, and the conscious mind has withdrawn itself and is totally unconscious to the external world. In the Delta State the mind goes from sleep and dreaming to a deep dreamless sleep state. At the Delta frequency, brainwaves are at their slowest, yet loudest, frequency, generated through deep meditation, deep sleep, or hypnotic trance. When the body is in the Delta frequency, awareness to the outside world is deferred and the body goes into a state of healing and rejuvenation, reprogramming and rebooting itself in preparation for operation upon awakening. At the Delta State there is no conscious awareness, and the mind is in a dreamless state. The Delta State is the vital to life's survival, and critical to the process of healing, fore it is in this state in which self-healing transpires.

The Beta state is our normal waking state. When we begin to lay down for bed and about to go to sleep we enter into a low beta state, drifting into an Alpha, daydreamy state just prior to falling asleep. As we slip off into our sleep, we smoothly transition from Alpha into the dreaming Theta state. As the body goes in and out the dream state throughout ones sleep, as the mind dreams in 90 minute cycles, the brain frequency dances back and forth between the dreamy Theta state, and the dreamless Delta state, counseling, healing and rejuvenating itself in preparation for operation upon awakening. The human body and mind work co-creatively, both directed by the spirit. Here we see the importance of having the Mind, Body, and Spirit in total alignment to produce a harmonious life and lifestyle. The alignment of the Mind, Body, and Spirit brings about an internal and external divine awareness of ones self, and ones relationship to the inside and outside world. Ones awareness, with right action and intent, can produce harmonious relationships with oneself, others, nature, and the surrounding environment. Mind, Body, Spirit alignment is critical to the survival, the healing, and the awakening process of each and every individual being.

Closely observing the brainwave activity, and the functions taking place at the various frequencies, through critical investigation, we begin to notice KEY information vital to our development and awareness of Self. At the levels of Alpha, Theta and Delta states, profound breakthroughs take place and occur, which in turn can be actualized in waking life. Through breath control we can consciously fluctuate our brainwave activity frequencies between states by simply speeding up, or slowing down, the breath in controlled cyclic breathing patterns. Through breathing and centering oneself in the awareness of the current moment, also known as meditation, one can elevate ones internal awareness (ie. knowledge, wisdom, understanding, what is happening in the mind, the body, the emotions, the spirit, the atmosphere, the planet, loved ones, distant places, other dimensions, Akashic Records, etc.). Now, by consciously accessing the various levels of awareness, and brainwave activity, one can begin to become aware of, and gain controlled access to, the human chakra and meridians system. The Chakra System is the energy system of the living human organism connecting the physical body to the spirit-energy enlivening, or living life, through and within that body. The Chakras offer opportunities to access energy portals of profound magnitudes, which in turn can be anchored and lived out on the physical plane. Accessing energy portals is opening oneself to energies already in existence within the self, which has, to a degree, or has not been previously, or currently, accessed by the individual. Meaning, one may be living life at a certain frequency (mind state, lifestyle, ideology, values, etc.) which may be considered "Low Frequency" which could be due to a variety of reasons. However, one day, the said individual living a "low frequency" life and lifestyle has a profound self-discovery moment which causes a unique feeling within the individual. That experience influenced chakra activity thruoughout the individual, on multiple levels/chakras, which produced the "unique feeling" as a result of the energetically interactive activity which took place within the individual, and between the individual, the atmosphere, and who or what it is that is being experienced by the individual...fore "As you experience a thing, the thing is simultaneously experiencing you." The highly profound breakthroughs often stimulate, or activate, the higher chakras on the energy system, while lower frequencies are stimulated by more physical activity and interactions. The Heart Chakra, which is in the area of the heart section of the body, is a key energetic meeting point on the human organism. The Heart Chakra is the meeting place for the Spirit and the Physical energy of the individual. It is also critical to balance the Heart Chakra in the Mind, Body, and Spirit alignment process, because all things (issues, thoughts, situations, circumstances, emotions, etc.) pass through the Heart Chakra for processing in the higher spheres. Harmonious alignment in the Heart Chakra renders smoother transitions to the higher levels of processing (even if one is unaware that the processing is happening). Unbalance in the Heart Chakra renders unbalance in ALL aspects of ones life, because the Heart Chakra houses and regulates ones Love frequency, as well as being central to life itself...one can continue to be alive though brain dead, but one cannot live heart dead. The heart area is central to life survival on the physical plane, fore it anchors and regulates the mind, body, and the spirit. With proper alignment, along with proper breath control, one can begin to regulate and reprogram ones mind, body, and spirit, engineering ones being through proper training and activity, to being the true and living divine beings we were intended to be on this great beautiful star, Earth.

Lesson 12

WHAT IS REIKI???

((Japanese word))   ((*English translation*))

    Rei   =   meaning *"God's Wisdom" (or) "The Higher Power"*

    Ki   =   meaning *"Life-Force Energy"*

Thus, Reiki ultimately means the practice of:

    "Life-Force Energy Guided By The Higher Power".

Reiki is quite simply a natural and safe method of healing which utilizes the body's natural healing abilities to stimulate healing and improvement on multiple levels. Reiki operates not only on the physical level, but also on the emotional, mental, and spiritual levels as well. Reiki is often incorporated into wellness at various points throughout the healing process of an individual. Reiki is an easy and relaxing approach to healing and wellbeing and balancing the brain hemispheres, and helps to not only stimulate healing in the body on multiple levels, but also encourage self-improvement and balance self-development in the process of manifesting ones greatest Self. When undergoing therapy, healing, and/or recovery many Reiki practitioners and Reiki-receivers have found that Reiki can be an excellent addition to the healing process! Reiki has been known to help speed up the healing process, as well as calm and comfort the body of the individual going through healing and/or recovery.   One of the beauties of the Reiki healing system is that it works well with other medical and therapeutic techniques, and often helps to relieve many of the side-effects of medications, and promotes harmonious recovery.

Reiki is Spiritual in Nature, and is not dependent upon any belief system at all...Reiki will do what it does regardless to ones belief; however if one is more receptive to the Reiki energy then the healing energy of Reiki can be more readily and rapidly integrated into the healee's energy body to work its effects out harmoniously without restriction. If one is skeptic or doubting the capacity and/or the reality of Reiki energy then one is only restricting ones own energy to the reception of the healing energy, which in turn slows down the healing process (similar to filling a swimming pool with an eye-dropper vs. a water-hose...its still filling the pool either way, its just one way is more productive than the other).

 SENSATIONS YOU MAY FEEL:::
Serene Peace/ At One with Your Self / At One with The Universe / Tingling in the body / Warmth / Light 'Buzzy' feeling / May fall asleep / Out of this world / Joy / Memories may surface / Extreme Relaxation / Extreme Happiness / Love / Clearing out of the old / Stepping into the new / Realization / Awakening / Refreshed / etc...

Both committed Reiki Masters and Practitioners alike make an active commitment to improve oneself daily via the Reiki Principles, which are as follows:

The secret art of inviting happiness, the miraculous medicine of all diseases...

Just For Today, Do Not Anger
Just For Today, Do Not Worry
Just For Today, Be Filled With Gratitude
Just For Today, Devote Yourself to Your Work (make an honest living)
Just For Today, Be Kind To All People.

Lesson 13

CULTIVATING AND NURTURING YOUR CHI ENERGY

As mentioned earlier, Chi is Life-Force Energy and therefore is vital to ones wellbeing and livelihood. A body without liveliness is just a flesh puppet orbiting throughout space... where is the Life and Joy in that? Ones liveliness branches out from ones sense of purpose and self-esteem. To get to the core of ones purpose and self-esteem it is necessary to look at ones own Spiritual Concept (or lack there of depending on the individual)...how one sees God or the Higher Power/Great Spirit. How one sees God (or The Divine Power) will give birth to the way one sees ones self, as well how one interprets life experiences and perceptions. How one sees God (or the Divine Power) and/or Self will assist to establish ones value system and determine what one sees as correct, right, balanced and/or divine. As you see this (how one sees God) can give way to a myriad of expressions and creativity and perspectives in the world. By focusing on the creative power within the individual (oneself) one can harness and nurture ones own creative energy…also known as Chi, Prana, Ki, Orgone Energy, Life-Force, Animism, etc. By nurturing your Chi one gains a greater sense of self and connectivity to the universe, oneself, and others, also filling ones body and spirit with life-stimulating energy bringing on great senses of serenity, peace, grounded, confidence, positivity, and clarity. Think for a moment how you feel when you visit an ocean shoreline, a waterfall, walk through the grass barefoot, relaxing in the sun… Doesn't it feel AMAZING!?! Times like these it feels like that's what the human race is here to do…simply enjoy Life! Enjoying Life entails experiencing all aspects Life offers you harmoniously in the present and/or upon reflection. Enjoying Life includes enjoying All Life (humanity and life beings, the elements, insects, animals, cosmic life and the cosmos, planetary life and planets, plants, atomic structures, minerals and All! There is no stone left out of the Light of Life! Let Love encompass all in your endeavors and journey throughout this Star (Earth). There are a variety of ways in which you can stimulate and nurture your Chi.

Ways To Replenish Your Chi::: Follow a natural and wholesome nutritious diet.
- EAT: Fruits, Vegetables, Nuts, Alkaline Foods (non-acidic foods)
- DON'T EAT: No (little) Meat, No Acidic Foods, No Acidic Drinks

Ways to Conserve Your Chi::: Practice Moderation (balance/non-overindulgence).
- BALANCE: Drinking, Sexual Activity, Sensual Gratification, Pleasures of all kinds, Emoting (dramatic/emotional outbursts) etc.

Ways to Secure Free-Flow of Chi::: Self-Awareness/Healing and Mindfulness.

- Periodic Fasting, Meditations, Breathing Techniques, Nature Walks, etc.
- Self-Expression and being free of emotional suppression (when/where necessary)

Above are ways in which one can balance the Elements (Fire, Water, Earth, Air) within the body, and their various modes, phases, and forms of expression. The Elements are often represented and reflected in the body system and its functions.

Fire is representative of the Mind, the imagination, and its creative ability to catch an idea or thought and take to creating its form (physical expression) like a wildfire.

Water is representative of the body's fluid system and the blood (Life-Force) that circulates throughout the body cleansing and vitalizing the body with Life Energy, and the human ability to take shape of its environment and/or adaptability capacity.

Air is representative of the oxygen we breathe and the words we speak. Mixing the words with imagination is like mixing fire and air... when the two meet, it only increases in power and ability and outward expression!

Earth is representative of the physical body, the form, and the plane upon which things manifest and take form.

All Elements are represented in the human system, and are necessary to be kept in balance to maintain a healthy lifestyle and positive wellbeing. The Elements can be kept in balance and harmony by following a carefully balanced lifestyle which integrates mindfulness practices with everyday living. By incorporating mindfulness to your everyday routine you will notice an increase in awareness and appreciation living in the moment, as well as feeling more at ease and at peace with yourself and surroundings while carrying out your daily duties. Mindfulness, when practiced regularly, brings about a total appreciation and serenity within oneself which connects one to not only oneself on a deeper level, but also deepens our relationships with others, infusing the individual with a greater sense of appreciation for all Life.

Lesson 14

DIGEST:

SELF-ACTUALIZE NOW!

Now, it's on you. From here on it will be of the most importance to Self-

Actualize right now! To be, and continue to become, your greatest self,

now. Right now. There is no time to waste... Each day you put off your

aspirations, is a missed opportunity, and potentially an opportunity lost.

Taking advantage of the Now, recognizing the power IN the Now

(getting up now, the thoughts you hold now after reading this, etc.), each day is a growing and opportunity for expansion. We can change daily if we allow ourselves...we can grow daily if we pay attention...the only cost is your awareness...taking the time to be aware in the moment, in the Now, and follow that positive shining little voice speaking your hearts desire...the drive that wakes you up each day... Remember how ambitious you were as a child, as a youth? Now and again we'll see our reflections in the youth today, reminding us of our own ambitions, and well as the voice in our heads chiming to testimony of 'if we chased our dreams or not'... and if we haven't IT'S NEVER TOO LATE. You are time. If 'we *are time*' then we must use *our time* constructively building our aspired realities, outlining and carving out our life experiences as we see fit, as we so choose...freely and creatively like the Atom. This life is yours, and your life is this (what you are experiencing now)... if you don't like what you see, create something new...and if you like what you are experiencing in life, elevate it even higher! There is no end! Live Now! Love Now! Be in the Now! Right Now!

Thank you for taking this time to be here now, and being you!

Peace, Love, and Light!

Odalo M. Wasikhongo

ACKNOWLEDGMENTS

My Mother

My Father

Jerry Miller Master Teacher

Sandra Fraser Master Teacher

Intelligent Mathematics my Enlightener, and the Gods and Earths of C-Medina

Michael Hawkeye Wilson Lightworker

Gini of Wisconsin Shaman Healer

Deon Daniel Lightworker

Edward Hinsman Lightworker of Wisconsin

Patrice Lightworker from when we were working in Hollywood

Linda & John of Sarasota, FL Crystal Dealer Lightworkers

Nathan of Minas Gerais, Brazil Crystal Dealer Lightworker

ALL LIGHTWORKERS!

ALL CRYSTAL, GEM, and/or METAPHYSICAL SHOPS!

ALL PEOPLE STRIVING for their Greatness and expression of their Truth

All Nurturers, Healers, Artists, Doctors, Protectors, Mothers, and Fathers

Members & Subscribers of my Freeing The Minds Channels on YouTube.com

Purchasers of this book

All Life

THANK YOU ALL!

CPSIA information can be obtained
at www.ICGtesting.com
Printed in the USA
FSOW04n0725130117
29179FS

9 780984 520312